Copyright © 2007 by Chronicle Books LLC.
All rights reserved.

Book design by Sara Gillingham.
Text by Traci N. Todd.
Typeset in Golden Ticket.
Manufactured in China.

Library of Congress Cataloging-in-Publication Data
C is for caboose : riding the rails from A to Z.
p. cm.
ISBN-13: 978-0-8118-5643-0
ISBN-10: 0-8118-5643-7
1. Railroads—Trains—Juvenile literature. 2. Alphabet—Juvenile literature.
TF148.C22 2007
385—dc22
2006018952

Distributed in Canada by Raincoast Books
9050 Shaughnessy Street, Vancouver, British Columbia V6P 6E5

10 9 8 7 6 5 4 3 2 1

Chronicle Books LLC
680 Second Street, San Francisco, California 94107

www.chroniclekids.com

C IS FOR CABOOSE

Canadian Pacific

437270

RIDING THE RAILS FROM A TO Z

chronicle books · san francisco

All aboard!

BOXCAR

a train car shaped like a box that carries things like grain, airplane parts, and clothing

BULLET TRAIN

a group of super-fast trains invented in Japan

BIG BOYS

the largest steam locomotives ever built

CABOOSE

the last car of a freight train

CIRCUS TRAIN

a train that carries circus animals, performers, and equipment

DEPOT

a building where trains stop to be loaded and unloaded

DINING CAR

a train's restaurant

ENGINEER

the person who drives the train

ENGINE

the part of the train
that gives it power

FLYING SCOTSMAN

a passenger train that has run between London, England, and Edinburgh, Scotland, since 1862

FAIR

the 1933 World's Fair in Chicago, Illinois, where people saw exciting new trains

WORLD'S FAIR CHICAGO

MAY 27 to NOV. 1 1933

SPECIAL REDUCED RAIL FARES

Travel CANADIAN PACIFIC

FAST CONVENIENT TRAIN SERVICE

GOLDEN SPIKE

used to celebrate the completion of the first railroad
to go all the way across the United States

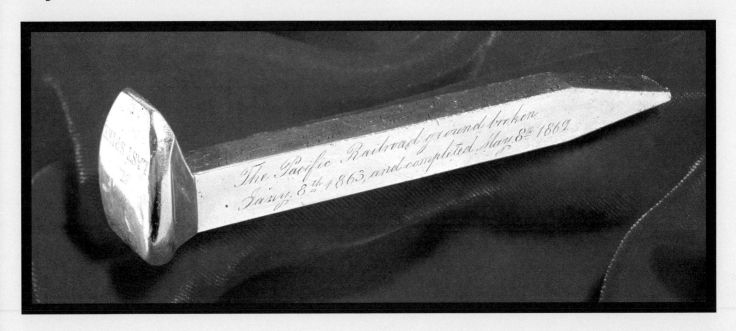

GEORGE PULLMAN

whose company, in the 1800s,
became famous for building
fancy railroad cars for people
to sleep in

HANDCAR
used to inspect the railroad tracks

H

HOSPITAL TRAIN
a hospital on wheels first used to care
for soldiers during the American Civil War

IMMIGRANTS

people from all over the world, especially Ireland and China, who helped build America's railroads

IRON HORSE

a nickname for trains, because before trains, horses were the fastest way to travel

JUNCTION
a place where two or more railroad tracks cross

JOHN HENRY
a folk hero who hammered a train tunnel through a mountain faster than a machine

KING'S CROSS
A large train station in London, England

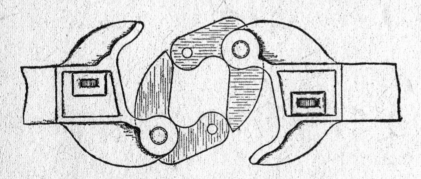

KNUCKLE COUPLER
connects the cars of a train

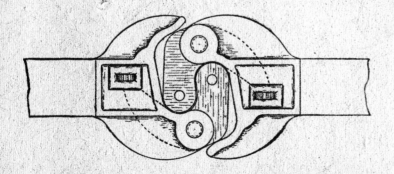

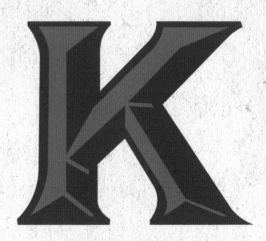

LOCOMOTIVE

the name for the train's engine and the part
of the train that pushes or pulls the cars

M-10000
a fancy, lightweight Union Pacific Railroad train that first appeared in the 1930s

MONORAIL
a train that runs on a single track

NEWSPAPER
that some people read while riding the train

NIGHT TRAIN
a train that runs at night and usually has cars for people to sleep in

OPEN-TOP HOPPER
a freight car with no roof that has openings underneath called "hoppers" for unloading freight

OIL
used to keep a train running smoothly

PIGGYBACK

to carry a truck trailer on the back of a flat train car

POSTER

this one advertised the Union Pacific Railway

QUICK

before there were
airplanes, trains
were the fastest
way to travel

ROUTE

the path a train takes from here to there

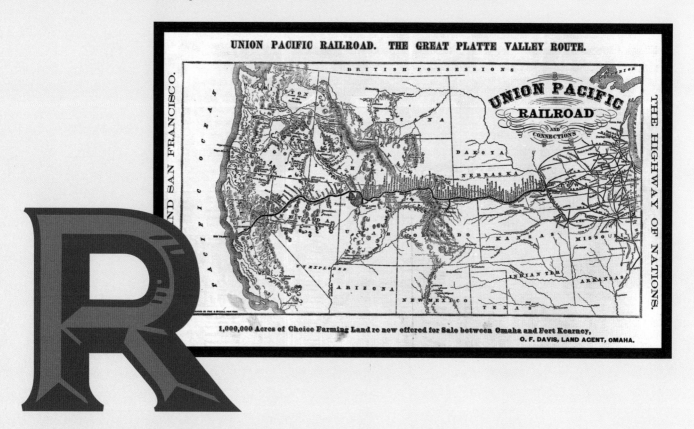

R

ROLLER COASTER

a train that sometimes does loop-de-loops

SCHOOL CAR

a traveling train car set
up like a classroom for
students who didn't have
schools in their hometowns

T

TUNNEL
a passageway built through a mountain

TICKET
for a seat on the train

TROLLEY
a streetcar that is powered by electricity and runs on rails

SERVES ALL THE WEST

UNION PACIFIC RAILROAD COMPANY
the largest railroad system in the United States

UNDERGROUND
the name for the subway in London, England

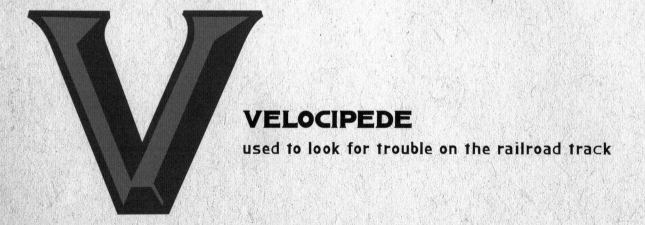

VELOCIPEDE

used to look for trouble on the railroad track

W

WHISTLE

engineers use it to warn people
and talk to other train workers

X

stands for "crossing"—a place where trains cross roads or sidewalks

YARD
a place where train cars are stored and repaired

YOSEMITE VALLEY RAILROAD
a small California railroad that ran to Yosemite National Park

ZEPHYR
a group of sleek Burlington
Railroad trains that first
appeared at the 1933–1934
World's Fair in Chicago

IMAGE CREDITS